The Life and World of

JOHN LENNON

Brian Williams

Heinemann
LIBRARY

www.heinemann/library.co.uk
Visit our website to find out more information about Heinemann Library books.

To order:
☎ Phone 44 (0) 1865 888066
📄 Send a fax to 44 (0) 1865 314091
💻 Visit the Heinemann Library Bookshop at www.heinemann/library.co.uk to browse our catalogue and order online.

First published in Great Britain by Heinemann Library, Halley Court, Jordan Hill, Oxford
OX2 8EJ, part of Harcourt Education.
Heinemann is a registered trademark of Harcourt Education Ltd.

Editorial: Lucy Thunder and Helen Cox
Design: Ron Kamen and Celia Floyd
Illustrations: Jeff Edwards and Joanna Brooker
Picture Research: Rebecca Sodergren and Elaine Willis
Production: Séverine Ribierre

Originated by Ambassador Litho Ltd
Printed in Hong Kong, China
by Wing King Tong

ISBN 0 431 14783 3
07 06 05 04 03
10 9 8 7 6 5 4 3 2 1

British Library Cataloguing in Publication Data
Williams, Brian
Life and world of John Lennon
782.4'2'166'092

A full catalogue record for this book is available from the British Library.

Acknowledgements
The Publishers would like to thank the following for permission to reproduce photographs:
Bettmann/Corbis p. **5**; Bubbles p. **28**; Camera Press pp. **6, 8, 9, 14, 24, 25, 26**; Corbis pp. **15, 16, 17, 18, 21, 20**; Tom Hanley p. **22**; Hulton Deutsch Collection/Corbis p. **23**; Hulton Getty pp. **7, 10, 13**; Pictorial Press p. **19**; Popperfoto p. **27**; Redferns p. **11**; Tracks p. **12**.

Cover photograph of John Lennon, reproduced with permission of RETNA/Michael Putland.

The Publishers would like to thank Rebecca Vickers for her assistance in the preparation of this book.

Every effort has been made to contact copyright holders of any material reproduced in this book. Any omissions will be rectified in subsequent printings if notice is given to the Publishers.

Contents

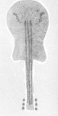

Any words shown in the text in bold, **like this**, are explained in the Glossary.

A pop hero

John Lennon was one of the Beatles, the most successful band in the history of pop music. Things happened to him that most people only dream about: he became a pop star in his twenties, he played guitar and sang to vast audiences of screaming fans and he became very rich. Yet, for John, this did not seem enough. His life ended tragically in 1980 when he was shot dead by a man claiming to be one of his fans.

Hero or rebel?

What does the life of John Lennon tell us about the world he lived in? To many young people he was a hero. They admired him for his music, for being a **rebel** and for his **campaigns** for peace and other causes. Other people pointed out that John Lennon was no saint. He behaved foolishly at times, took harmful drugs, broke the law and upset his friends. Success and fame did not always bring happiness. Few of his fans knew much about the private side of this famous man. To them, he was just John, one of the 'fab four' – the Beatles.

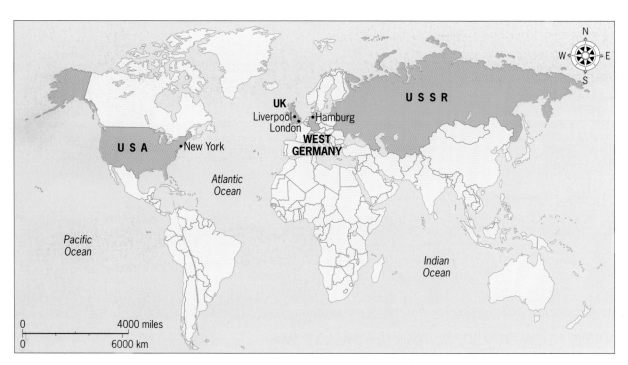

▲ John Lennon grew up in a world recovering from war. Britain had given up its **empire**. The world's strongest nation was the USA, the country whose music had first inspired John Lennon. The USA was where he finally made his home.

In his own words

We know a lot about John Lennon, from his own writings and songs. We can read and watch media reports of his life, covering four **decades** (the 1940s to the 1970s). These were years of great changes in Britain, when John Lennon was part of a youthful **revolution**. That is one reason why people still listen to his music and remember his life and times.

▶ This photo of John Lennon was taken in 1968, with his son Julian and Yoko Ono. Today John Lennon would be a grandfather, in his 60s. What would he think of the world he helped to shape?

Key dates

1940	John Lennon is born in Liverpool
1958	John's mother is killed in a road accident
1962	John marries Cynthia Powell
1962	The Beatles have their first chart success
1963	John's son Julian is born
1968	John and Cynthia are **divorced**
1969	John marries Yoko Ono
1970	The Beatles break up
1975	John's son Sean is born
1980	John Lennon is murdered in New York

War baby

John Lennon was born on 9 October 1940 in Liverpool in England. He was a 'war baby', for Britain had been at war (World War II) since 1939. John was given the middle name of Winston, after Britain's wartime leader, Winston Churchill.

John's family

Liverpool is a port and many people in the city had links with the sea and ships. John's mother, Julia Stanley, was the daughter of a sailmaker, and his father, Freddie, worked as a seaman.

Freddie Lennon's seafaring took him away from Liverpool for months at a time, and the Lennons' marriage suffered. Julia found it hard to bring up her baby son alone. In 1941 she handed him over to her sister, Mary, whom John called Aunt Mimi. Mary lived with her husband, George Smith, in a semi-detached house in a Liverpool suburb called Woolton.

Wartime Britain

Like other British cities, Liverpool was bombed by German planes. John had been born during an **air raid**. During World War II, thousands of people were killed and many homes were destroyed by falling bombs. Food and clothing were **rationed**. At night there was a **blackout**. The war lasted six years (1939 to 1945), and John was nearly five before peace returned.

◀ This photo shows the young John Lennon at home. It was taken by his Aunt Mimi.

Wartime Britain had become the temporary home for soldiers, sailors and airmen from all over the world. Many were Americans, who brought chocolate, chewing gum and their music – jive, jazz and big-band dance music. Among the Americans were black soldiers. **Liverpudlians** were used to seeing black faces in their port city (Liverpool had a small black population). But for many Britons, the American soldiers were the first black people they had ever seen.

▲ These men are cleaning up after a bombing raid on Liverpool during World War II. Liverpool was a target because of its busy port, which attracted ships from all over the world.

Making the best of it

As a child, John knew hard times. Many foods, such as eggs, butter and meat, were scarce because of the war and so were **rationed**. You could only buy one egg a week, for example. Sugar was 'like gold-dust' and bananas vanished from the shops. People carried on as best they could. Everyone listened to the radio (the 'wireless') for war news. They also enjoyed radio comedy shows and music played by dance bands. Many people went to the cinema at least once a week.

Growing up in Liverpool

I n 1945, the war ended. There were parades and street parties to celebrate victory and the return of peace. John was a happy child, ready for school.

Problems of peace

Then his father, Freddie, returned from his latest job on a ship. He now wanted John to live with him. John's mother said no; John was better off with Aunt Mimi and Uncle George. It was an upsetting time.

Britain was battered after six years of war. Cities and factories were in ruins. Many families had lost homes to German bombs. It was time to rebuild. People voted for change in the 1945 **general election**. The new **Labour** government promised free hospitals, better schools and more new homes.

John's interests

At John's first school, Dovedale Primary School in Liverpool, the teachers sometimes found him difficult. He was happy at home, but missed his mother. He was clever but could be a bully. John liked drawing and loved reading funny, but strange, comics and books, such as Lewis Carroll's *Alice's Adventures in Wonderland*.

▲ John outside the house where he grew up in Menlove Avenue, Woolton.
It was a typical middle-class home – his friends thought it a bit 'posh'.

In February 1952, Britain's King George VI died and the young Princess Elizabeth became queen. That year, aged eleven, John passed an exam to go to Quarry Bank High School. Out of school, he liked listening to American music, especially **blues** and country music. In 1956, Aunt Mimi bought him a guitar. His mother, Julia (who played the banjo), liked American music, too. John and three schoolfriends formed a **skiffle** group, calling themselves the Quarrymen.

▲ The Quarrymen played at a Woolton church fete on 6 July 1957. A friend introduced John to a boy who played guitar left-handed. John soon asked him to join the band. The new boy was Paul McCartney.

Britain enters a new age

In 1953, Queen Elizabeth II was crowned in Westminster Abbey. For the first time, millions of people watched the **coronation** on television. More people could now afford TVs, cars, washing machines and refrigerators. In the new Britain, there were growing numbers of **immigrants** from the West Indies, India and Pakistan. Most of the newcomers found work and homes in cities, because Britain needed more workers to help rebuild the country after the war.

The Beatles are born

Teenager John had to think about a career. In the 1950s, most young people found it easy to get jobs after school, though only a few went on to university. In 1957, John moved to Liverpool College of Art. Cynthia Powell, another student, became his girlfriend. He liked art, but dreamed of becoming a pop singer.

The BBC hardly played any pop records. John and his friends tuned in their radios to Radio Luxembourg, which played the kind of American rock 'n' roll music they liked. A new guitarist joined John's band: fourteen-year-old George Harrison.

Goodbye to Liverpool

On 15 July 1958, Julia Lennon was killed, after being hit by a car outside John's home. She was only 44. The death of his mother was a terrible shock to John – 'the worst thing that happened to me,' he said later.

▲ Teenagers listen to music at a record shop listening booth. By 1960, young people in Britain had enough money to follow fashion and buy the latest hits. Record sales were rising fast.

In 1960, John gave up his college course. The Quarrymen were getting paid to play at clubs and dances. He just wanted to make music, and the band switched from 'twangy' **skiffle** to 'thumping' rock 'n' roll, copying the American sounds John liked. John and Paul wrote songs together. After some argument, the Quarrymen picked a new name: the Beatles. Alongside John and Paul were George, John's friend Stuart Sutcliffe and drummer Pete Best. In August 1960, the five Beatles left Liverpool and crossed the North Sea to Germany. They had been booked to play at the Star Club in Hamburg. John was nineteen.

▲ This photograph shows the Beatles in Hamburg. From left to right: Pete Best, George Harrison, John Lennon, Paul McCartney, Stuart Sutcliffe.

Teenage Britain

Like other teenagers, John and his friends went to the 'pictures' (the cinema) and met girls at dances and coffee bars. Hardly anyone they knew had a car, so they went everywhere by bus or bike, or walked. At home, they watched TV, which at that time was still only broadcast in black and white. Teenagers spent money on records (singles and long-playing vinyl **albums**). They liked clothes that made them look different from adults, such as pointed 'winkle-picker' shoes.

On the way up

Hamburg was a tough port city, like Liverpool. Night after night, the Beatles played loud pop music to noisy club audiences. They ate junk food, drank too much and took drugs for the first time, to keep themselves awake.

Back in Liverpool

By January 1961, they were back in Liverpool, without Stuart Sutcliffe, who stayed in Germany. At home, the remaining Beatles made their first appearance at the Cavern, a popular club for pop music fans. John wrote about the Beatles for a local pop paper, *Mersey Beat*, adding poems and cartoons of his own.

In late 1961, a Liverpool record shop manager named Brian Epstein heard the band play. He became the Beatles' manager. Epstein gave them a new 'image'. The Beatles swopped their black leather stage outfits for grey suits and had their hair cut into shaggy mops.

► The front page of this 1962 issue of *Mersey Beat* magazine shows the four Beatles. John (second from left) hoped their new image, and manager Brian Epstein, would bring them success.

THE NORTH'S OWN ENTERTAINMENTS PAPER

MERSEY BEAT

FRANK HESSY

BEATLES RECORD FOR EMI
story inside

WE ARE NOW ACCEPTING ORDERS FOR
THE BEATLES
FIRST RECORD ON PARLOPHONE
LOVE ME DO
c/w
P.S. I LOVE YOU
RELEASED FRIDAY OCTOBER 5th

ODD SPOT CLUB
89 BOLD STREET
LIVERPOOL

Regrouping for the big time

Epstein arranged for the Beatles to play for George Martin, a producer at a London record company. Martin liked the Beatles' sound, but did not think their drummer was good enough. Pete Best was replaced by Ringo Starr (whose real name was Richard Starkey).

John now had personal concerns, too. Cynthia was pregnant. In August 1962, she and John were married. He was 21. Two weeks later, the Beatles were recording in a London studio. In October, their first single 'Love Me Do' was released. It got to number 17 in the Top 20 chart. The Beatles were on their way. John Lennon was about to become the star he had always wanted to be.

▲ In Britain and other countries, people took part in 'Ban the Bomb' marches. This photo shows supporters of the Campaign for Nuclear Disarmament (CND) at a **protest rally** in London. They were calling for all countries to get rid of nuclear weapons.

Changing and dangerous times

In 1960, the USA had a new young President, John F. Kennedy. In 1961, Yuri Gagarin of the **USSR** became the first person to fly in space. Times were changing, but they were also scary. Many people feared a new world war. The USA and the USSR were rivals, and each side had thousands of rockets and **nuclear weapons**. The two 'superpowers' nearly went to war in 1962 over Russian rockets on the Caribbean island of Cuba, close to the USA. Luckily, the 'Cuban Missile Crisis' ended without war; the Russians took away their rockets.

Pleasing the world

'Please Please Me', the Beatles' first chart-topping record, came out in January 1963. It was followed in May by the band's first **album** (which had the same title). When the Beatles toured Britain, often playing in cinemas, young fans screamed and shouted; they loved the Beatles' music.

John becomes a father

In April 1963, John and Cynthia's son was born in Liverpool. They named the baby John Charles Julian Lennon. The birth, like John's marriage, was kept a secret. Newspapers and fans must not know that 'wacky John' was now a married man and a father.

▼ John with his wife Cynthia and baby son Julian. The Beatles' private lives were hidden from their fans. John Lennon, husband and father, was not the image the Beatles' manager wanted the world to see.

'Beatlemania'

In June 1963, the band appeared on television in their own series. They performed for the last time at Liverpool's Cavern club in August, and in November they were on stage in London, singing in front of the royal family. Fans mobbed them whenever they appeared. John and Paul were compared with great music composers of the past. The *Daily Mirror* newspaper made up a word to describe the craziness: 'Beatlemania'. Only the death of President Kennedy in November 1963 pushed the Beatles off the front pages.

John loved being a star. For the next two years, every record the Beatles made was a hit. They became known as the 'fab four'. In February 1964, they toured the USA where they caused a sensation. The four appeared on American TV, where John's wit (and Liverpool accent) baffled American interviewers. In March 1964, John published a book called *In His Own Write*, and began working on the Beatles' first film *A Hard Day's Night*. The pace was fast and furious.

▼ The USA went wild over the Beatles. Thousands of teenagers packed airports to greet them. Concerts sold out and fans chased them everywhere they went.

A public murder

US President John F. Kennedy was shot dead while visiting Dallas, Texas on 22 November 1963. People everywhere were shocked by his murder. The world seemed suddenly more dangerous for famous people.

A hard day's night

John and the other Beatles were working so hard, they barely knew what time it was. The title of their first film, *A Hard Day's Night*, probably sums up what it felt like. In 1965, they made a second film, *Help!* Each Beatle had now been given a 'character': George was quiet, Ringo funny, Paul lovable, while John was 'smart'. His second book, *A Spaniard in the Works*, was a bestseller.

The British are coming

British pop and British fashions were copied in the USA and around the world. Liverpool had become famous for pop music, while London's shops sold the new clothes that the pop stars helped to show off. Other British pop and rock groups, such as the Rolling Stones and The Who, were making headlines, too.

In 1965, trying to win popularity by seeming 'cool', the British government gave the Beatles **MBE** awards. John said: 'I thought you had to drive a tank and win wars to get an MBE.' People wrote to the newspapers complaining that it was wrong to honour young pop stars in this way, and some holders of MBEs returned their awards in protest.

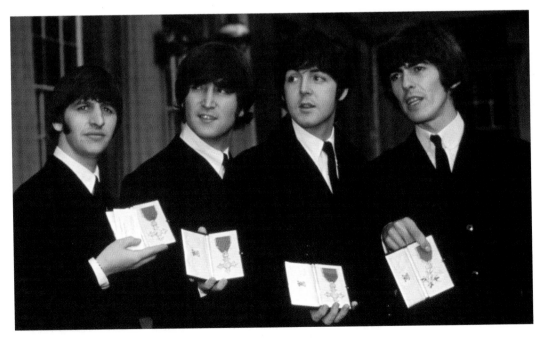

▲ The Beatles received their MBE awards from the Queen at Buckingham Palace. John (second from the left) shows off his medal, along with Ringo, Paul and George.

John causes an upset

John told a newspaper reporter that the Beatles were more popular than Jesus. He meant that fewer people were going to church, but his words shocked many Christians. When the Beatles returned to the USA in 1966, they were sent death threats. Protesters burned their records. John now knew that superstars had to be careful not to upset their fans.

▼ Swinging Britain came to a solemn halt in January 1965 for the funeral of Sir Winston Churchill. Britain's leader during World War II had died at the age of 90.

Swinging London

In the 1960s, fashion designers, such as Mary Quant, made London the centre of the youth fashion scene. Young people went to shops in London's Carnaby Street and King's Road to buy mini (very short) skirts and other trendy clothes. The world loved British pop music, especially bands such as the Beatles and the Rolling Stones, and British youth fashion. Sixties Britain was 'swinging' (cool).

Help!

John played his last Beatles' concert in Britain, at Wembley, in May 1966. The band's last-ever public concert took place in San Francisco, USA, in August 1966. Performing in huge arenas in front of thousands of yelling fans was no longer fun. 'It was just a sort of freak show,' John explained: 'The only reason to be Beatles is to make music, and not just be in a circus.' No one could hear the music anyway.

Success and all it buys...

John was by now so rich that he could buy whatever he wanted – cars, televisions, houses. Yet he was not happy. In 1966 he had met a Japanese artist named Yoko Ono. She became his companion. His marriage was failing. He later said that his song title 'Help!' summed up how low he felt.

He put his energy into the new Beatles' **album**. It took 700 hours of recording studio work. The result was 'Sgt Pepper's Lonely Hearts Club Band'. Everyone said it was the Beatles' best.

◄ These fans, at one of the last Beatles concerts in New York in 1966, were described by John as coming to watch a 'freak show'.

...does not always bring happiness

In August 1967, Brian Epstein was found dead from a drug **overdose**. He had held the Beatles together. Without him, John and the others began to drift apart. They set up a record company named Apple, but it began to lose money and there were more arguments.

John spent more time writing his own songs. He tried the powerful drug **LSD**. He went off to India to explore Eastern religion. In November 1968, he and Cynthia were **divorced**. John and Yoko shared their ideas for new music and art. The two also made news for the wrong reasons, when they were arrested for having an illegal drug, **cannabis**.

▲ The Beatles visited India to study Eastern religion. With their girlfriends, they sat around the Maharishi Mahesh Yogi. His teachings were a mixture of ideas from Hinduism and Buddhism.

Protests and violence

1968 was a year of student protest in the USA and Europe. The protests were mostly about US involvement in the **Vietnam War**. Anti-war protests around the world led to marches and **rallies** in cities. It seemed that young people everywhere were leading a **revolution**. John even wrote a song called 'Revolution'. Peace and love, words common in pop songs of the time, were hard to find.

Breaking up

By 1969, after eight years, the Beatles had come to the end of the road. John wanted to record either solo (on his own) or with Yoko. One of his first solo hits was 'Give Peace a Chance'. In 1969, John returned his **MBE**, to **protest** (he said) about Britain's support for the USA's war in Vietnam and its part in the civil **war** in Nigeria.

John and Yoko recorded an **album**. The cover was banned, because it showed the two of them naked. They made films, too – one showed John's smiling face, for 52 minutes. Beatles fans did not really understand what John was trying to say.

▲ John and Yoko talk to journalists in bed. 'Bed-ins' did not change the world, but John's **campaigns** inspired other pop stars to support causes.

The peace campaigner

In March 1969, John and Yoko were married in Gibraltar. They staged a strange 'bed-in' in their room at the Amsterdam Hilton Hotel in the Netherlands. They sat in bed, talking to journalists and photographers about world peace. John really thought that pop music could change the world for the better.

John changed his name to John Ono Lennon and set up home with Yoko. In 1970, the Beatles made their last film *Let it Be* and their last album, 'Abbey Road'. Paul McCartney was first to say in public that 'the Beatles have left the Beatles'. John had already made the break. A new **decade** was beginning, and a new period in John's life. He was now 30 years old.

▲ Technology was bringing new wonders. US President Kennedy had promised to send Americans to the moon before the 1960s ended. In 1969 the world watched on television as the USA's Apollo 11 astronauts, Neil Armstrong and Edwin (Buzz) Aldrin, walked on the moon.

Flower power

As the 1970s began, many young people dreamed of a new society, based on peace and love. Students 'dropped out' of college to wear flowers in their long hair, listen to dreamy music and study Eastern religions (as John Lennon did). Some took drugs to 'expand their minds', in an attempt to see the world in a different light. Pop stars were blamed for encouraging drug abuse among young people.

Give peace a chance

As he grew older, John looked back on his life. He wrote songs about his mother. Now in his thirties, he felt disappointed that the hopes of the 1960s seemed to have vanished. The 'dream' was over. Singing 'Give Peace a Chance' had not changed the world.

Personal problems

John also had more personal problems. Yoko had been married before she met John, and had a daughter. The Lennons wanted to make her part of their family, but Yoko's ex-husband would not agree. The argument ended in the law courts. John and Yoko were briefly arrested on charges of kidnapping Yoko's daughter. In the early 1970s Yoko won the court battle, but did not get to see her daughter again until fairly recently.

John's peace **protests** were now beginning to bore people. Even taking your clothes off no longer caused a stir: actors in stage shows like *Oh Calcutta* and *Hair* did it all the time. The pop world had moved on, too. There were new bands, with new sounds, but John's song 'Imagine', recorded in July 1971, was a huge hit. In this song, John sang about an ideal world, the world that existed only in his imagination.

▲ John and Yoko at home working on John's 'Imagine' **album**. The title track from this album became his most famous song as a solo singer.

Looking to the USA

John felt no one in Britain took him seriously. He was happier in the USA. He was sure that he and Yoko would be respected there, as artists and **campaigners**. The US government, however, did not want the former Beatle to live in the USA. John had spoken out against the **Vietnam War**, and he had been arrested for having drugs. More trouble lay ahead for him.

▼ Attacks by the IRA left streets in London covered with debris after car bombs exploded in March 1973.

New money and bombs in the streets

The Britain John left behind was changing. In 1971 the country swapped its old pounds, shillings and pennies for decimal currency (based on 100 pennies to the pound). And in 1973, after years of trying, it finally joined the **European Community**. In 1973–74 the troubles in Northern Ireland brought fear and bloodshed to British cities like Birmingham and London, where the **IRA** exploded bombs that killed and injured people.

In the spotlight

In the USA, John and Yoko were in the news and on television a lot. They spoke out on **controversial** issues. They supported the civil rights campaigns of black Americans and Native Americans. They said that the British Army should leave Northern Ireland, and that US soldiers should leave Vietnam. Admirers praised their principles and courage. Enemies threatened to kill them and told them to leave the USA.

Unwelcome in the USA

John's **protests** alarmed the US government. Was John Lennon set on overturning the American way of life? If so, he was an unwelcome visitor. In 1973, John and Yoko moved into an apartment building in New York. They hoped to settle in the USA. The US government said that John could stay only a short while. So began a long argument in the law courts to stop John being removed from the USA.

▲ The World Trade Center was completed in New York City in 1973. The twin towers were the latest landmark in the city John Lennon wanted to make his new home. They would remain New York's tallest buildings, until destroyed by **terrorists** on 11 September 2001.

Life in the spotlight

Though the former Beatle was still popular, many Beatles fans had never taken to Yoko. Some blamed her for the Beatles' break-up. The Lennons were always in the spotlight. Like many celebrities, they were photographed wherever they went. This publicity put John and Yoko under strain. In 1973 they split up, and for a time John moved to Los Angeles in California. He had a new girlfriend.

Sunny California was a long way from chilly Britain, where during the winter of 1973–74 many schools and offices were lit by candles. This was because power stations were short of oil after a war in the Middle East. John had few ties now with his old homeland. In 1974, he played and sang live for the last time, with Elton John at a concert in New York. In 1975 John and Yoko got back together and he returned to New York. Soon there was good news: he was to become a father again.

▲ During the winter of 1973–74, many people in Britain worked by candle or gas lamps part of the time. Everyone was asked to save electricity and not drive their cars much either. Meanwhile, John was having a good time in California, with his new girlfriend, May Pang.

The power of television

By the mid-1970s, people were realizing just how powerful TV had become. Almost every home had a television, and satellites beamed live TV pictures of wars, protests and other major events around the world. Power cuts meant no TV for a few hours.

New Yorker

John and Yoko's son was born in October 1975. John was thrilled and said, 'I feel higher than the Empire State Building.' They named the baby Sean Taro Ono Lennon. At the age of 35, John was determined to be a good father to Sean.

John Lennon, house-husband

In 1976, the US government finally allowed John to remain in the USA. While Yoko took care of their business interests (they owned four farms and two yachts, among other things), John stayed at home. He had come to depend on Yoko, and had a pet name for her: 'Mother'. She managed his life.

▲ This photo of John Lennon with Yoko and his son Sean shows a happy father. He seemed to have found a new peace of mind.

John Lennon, pop star and protester, had become John Lennon, bread-maker and cat-lover. At times, he lived on cups of tea, brown rice and vegetables, wandering around at home without any clothes, listening to his vast record collection.

Back to work

From 1975 to 1980, there were no new John Lennon records. John was almost forgotten. The Beatles rarely met. Rumours about the four playing together again never became reality.

However, in 1980, John sailed his yacht to Bermuda, an adventure that made him keen to work again. He had more songs he wanted to sing. With Yoko, he recorded the **album** 'Double Fantasy'. Not everyone liked it, but John was keen to press on with his career.

On the afternoon of 8 December 1980, he came home from the recording studio. Waiting outside his apartment was a 25-year-old fan named Mark Chapman. John heard a voice call 'Mr Lennon!'. He turned. Chapman pulled out a gun and fired five times. Police rushed John to hospital, but he was dead by the time they got there.

▶ Mark Chapman (right) asked John Lennon for his autograph. Hours later he waited in the evening shadows and shot John dead, because, he claimed, the singer had not lived up to the ideals he sang about.

Shooting makes news

1980 was the year that fans of the popular US TV series *Dallas* waited to find out 'Who shot JR?'. (JR was one of the show's main characters.) However, real life was to bring real tragedies – Archbishop Romero was shot dead in El Salvador and pop star John Lennon was murdered in New York City. Three months after John's death, a gunman tried to shoot the USA's new president, Ronald Reagan.

John Lennon remembered

Fans all over the world mourned John Lennon. He is still remembered. For many, his songs remind them of the 1960s, when the Beatles shot to fame. Other people remember John Lennon as a man who wanted peace in the world. After he died, Americans held up posters reading 'No more guns' – a demand that continues today.

A hero after death?

Violent death makes heroes of some people. John Lennon's murder seemed pointless, like the shooting of President Kennedy in 1963. However, it brought John back into the spotlight. Radio stations played Lennon songs endlessly for weeks. Newspapers and TV traced his career from Liverpool to New York.

Why is Lennon remembered?

Later pop stars, including Bob Geldof, Sting, U2 and Geri Halliwell, followed John Lennon's lead and became **campaigners**. However, most of all, John Lennon is remembered for his music, not his campaigning. Lennon and McCartney were the most successful songwriters of the 20th century. Young musicians still copy the style of the Beatles' music today.

◄ People still listen to the music of John Lennon and the Beatles today. In 1995, fans rushed to buy previously unheard Beatles songs. Two songs written by John Lennon, 'Real Love' and 'Free as a Bird', were heard for the first time.

Coming home

During John Lennon's life, new technology (especially TV) changed the way people lived. Youth culture and pop music became international. John was a global star, his face instantly recognized by people in many countries.

In the end, John Lennon found peace at home, just as he'd sung in 1964, in a line from 'A Hard Day's Night': 'When I'm home, everything seems to be right.'

▲ John Lennon was often in front of a microphone and camera. When he wasn't singing, he was giving his views to the world. He said his job was 'to write for the people'.

The Beatles' records

The Beatles have sold more than 1 billion records. They had eleven number one hits in a row and seventeen UK chart-toppers (twenty in the USA). John Lennon wrote more than twenty-five number one songs.

Glossary

air raid   attack from the air by planes dropping bombs

album   collection of songs sold in a record shop; in John Lennon's day albums were on long-playing vinyl records

blackout   wartime ban on street lights, signs and lights shining from windows

blues   form of black American folk music

campaign   action by people who want to change laws, or make something happen

cannabis   drug made from a plant, also known as marijuana

civil war   war between two groups in the same country

controversial   causing a disagreement or upset

coronation   ceremony of crowning a new king or queen

decade   period of ten years

divorce   when a married couple end their marriage by legal agreement

empire   large area of land, ruled over by a single person or government

European Community   trading group set up in 1957; now the European Union

general election   voting for members of parliament. The winning party forms the new government

immigrants   people who move into another country to live

IRA   Irish Republican Army, a nationalist organization fighting for a united Ireland

Labour   name of one of the main political parties in Britain

Liverpudlian   someone from Liverpool

LSD   short for lysergic acid diethylamide, a drug which can make people see things in a dreamlike way and do odd or dangerous things

MBE   stands for Member of the British Empire, an award for public service

nuclear weapons   atomic and hydrogen bombs

overdose   taking more drugs than it is safe to, which can lead to death

protest   arguing against something you think is wrong

protest rally   gathering of people who have a common interest or view

rally   gathering of people who have a common interest or view

rationed   kept to an agreed amount, or ration; in wartime Britain people had ration coupons (like stamps) for certain items

rebel   person who opposes the system

revolution   sudden change, overthrow of old ideas

skiffle   country-style music often played on home-made instruments

terrorist   someone who uses violence for political gain

USSR   Union of Soviet Socialist Republics, Communist superstate that, until 1991, included Russia, Ukraine and other countries now independent

Vietnam War   war that began in the 1950s between Communist North and non-Communist South Vietnam. During the 1960s and early 1970s, US forces helped the South Vietnamese

Timeline

1940 John Lennon is born in Liverpool

1945 World War II ends

1953 Queen Elizabeth II's coronation

1960 The Beatles leave Liverpool to perform in Germany

1963 Beatles first top the pop charts with 'Please Please Me'

1963 President Kennedy is shot dead

1964 Beatles make their first film, *A Hard Day's Night*

1964 'Beatlemania' hits the USA

1966 England win soccer's World Cup

1969 First US astronauts land on the Moon

1970 Beatles make their last recordings as a group

1971 John Lennon's 'Imagine' album is released. The Lennons move to New York City.

1979 Margaret Thatcher becomes Britain's first woman prime minister

1980 John Lennon is murdered

1994 John Lennon is elected to the Rock and Roll Hall of Fame

2001 Beatle George Harrison dies

Further reading & websites

Profiles: John Lennon, Paul Dowswell (Heinemann Library, 2001)

Heinemann Explore – an online resource from Heinemann.
For Key Stage 2 history go to *www.heinemannexplore.co.uk*

http://www.legend-johnlennon.com/

http://cyber-beatles.com

Places to visit

John's boyhood home in Menlove Avenue, Liverpool
(owned by the National Trust)

The Beatles Story Museum, Liverpool

The Cavern Club, Liverpool (a replica of the original
Cavern Club, which was demolished in 1973)

The National Centre for Popular Music, Sheffield

The British Library, London (which has an exhibition of
original Beatles songs)

Index

Titles in the *Life and World Of* series include:

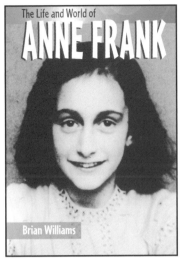

Hardback   0 431 14780 9

Hardback   0 431 14781 7

Hardback   0 431 14782 5

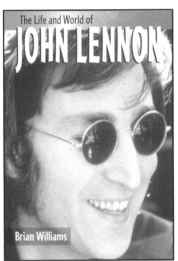

Hardback   0 431 14783 3

Hardback   0 431 14784 1

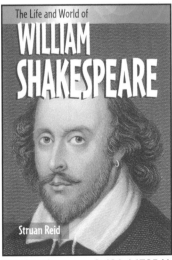

Hardback   0 431 14785 X

Find out about the other titles in this series on our website www.heinemann.co.uk/library